CREATORS NOT CONSUMERS
Rediscovering Social Education

NAYC Publications

Published by NAYC Publications
Keswick House, 30 Peacock Lane, Leicester LE1 5NY

First published August 1980.
Reprinted October 1980.
Second Edition January 1982.
Reprinted January 1983.

Graphics and typesetting by Overload of Leicester.

Printed by Overload of Leicester.

© Mark Smith

Extracts from this booklet may be reproduced for educational and training activities. Special permission for such uses is not required. We do, however, ask that the following statement appears on all reproductions:

> Reproduced from *Creators not Consumers* by Mark Smith.
> Published by NAYC Publications 1982.

This permission statement is limited to partial reproduction for educational or training events. Complete or systematic or large-scale reproduction – or inclusion of extracts in publications for sale may be done only with prior written permission.

All rights reserved.

ISBN 0 907095 02 X

Mark Smith is a tutor on the YMCA Distance Learning Project. He was the coordinator of the NAYC Political Education Project.

Introduction

This booklet has been written to promote discussion about social education. In the twenty years or so since the term first came into common usage there have been a number of developments in youth work thinking that have not been fully reflected in writing about social education. To show what this thinking means in practice I have looked at how a group of young people organised a club skating trip and from that developed a view of social education.

With stocks of the book once again running low, I have taken the opportunity to make some major additions to the text and update the reading list. Whilst the views expressed are my own, Bernard Davies, Angie Foister, Gina Ingram, Cathy Kirkwood, Rod Moore, Alan Rogers and Tony Taylor gave valuable advice and help. The Politics Association also allowed me to include part of an earlier article first published in *Teaching Politics*.

Mark Smith
November 1981

1. The ice skating trip

Just after club had finished Neil came into the office and asked if we could organise an ice skating trip. He thought we could easily fill a coach if we charged £1.50 per person. How did he arrive at £1.50 we asked? That's what the British Legion had charged. How many people had he spoken to? About half a dozen. In the end it was agreed that he should take a list around next club night to gauge the response. He got 45 names and a delegation trouped in, would we now organise the coach and book the rink? You do it, we suggest, and after some discussion they go away and decide on a date and sort out 'who is doing what'. Tony and Sue return, phone a bus company, and book a 42 seater. That's three less seats than people who said they wanted to go, we say, and anyway where are we going to sit? People are bound to drop out comes the answer. They leave a scribbled note for the secretary to type in the morning. Meanwhile Neil is out canvassing the choice of rink. "Silver Blades" is the most popular so Tony and Sue do their bit again. What are you going to charge? They'd clean forgotten to ask the cost of the coach. Another phone call and Mike (who was skillful with figures) produced the answer – £1.65 if we were going to allow a little leeway for those who didn't turn up on the day and to give a tip to the driver. Mike took responsibility for the deposits, giving them to us to bank.

Youth workers are always booking coaches and organising trips, young people aren't. It takes a lot of confidence, a fair bit of knowledge and quite complex skills to do what these young women and men did, yet they were all what could be called 'low stream secondary modern' and aged from 15 to 18 years. Take Neil for instance. When the workers first knew him he had considerable difficulties in relating to anyone in authority and often to his peers. His frequent violent out-bursts and apparent concern only for his own feelings had gained him the reputation of being a "right bastard" and posed the workers problems. It had taken two years to establish a comfortable relationship between Neil and the workers and what was significant about his suggestion of an ice skating trip was not so much that he had made it, but that he had taken responsibility to do something about it. The workers had therefore been very keen to respond to his suggestion.

In this first chapter I want to look at two frameworks that can help us understand why organising a skating trip in this way can be seen as social education. These frameworks are:

1. Youth work as process and product.
2. Knowledge, feelings and skills as elements of a problem.

Product and Process

These workers wanted to build up people's ability to do things for themselves. The way they went about doing this can be more clearly seen if we think of youth work as having processes and products. Processes are the way we use the different resources (or inputs) at our disposal. Products are the concrete events or things we create. Both products and processes have certain results. Thus we can show the ice skating trip in the form of the diagram. (See Figure 1.)

People put different emphasis on product and process. In general workers and administrators are keen on work that can be readily seen and counted. They are interested in concrete results from their efforts, such as the number of football teams a club fields, attendance on club nights or building usage.

Process results are far less tangible. They are to do with relationships, the strengthening of people's competence and feelings. Both product and process results can feed back into the inputs. Thus a financial loss on an activity, (a product result), might mean there is less money available for other events or the development of people's skills, (a process result), might mean a more involved 'activity' is possible.

If we return to the trip, the product result was an ice skating trip that in the end has 29 participants, a financial loss (£16) and left four members stranded in London when they did not turn up on time for the returning coach (the decision of the organisers). It is not an outcome that recommends itself to youth work administrators keen to justify their work by the usual standards. Some of the process (or educational) results can be seen when the members organised another trip – they

Figure 1 **Product and Process in the Skating Trip**

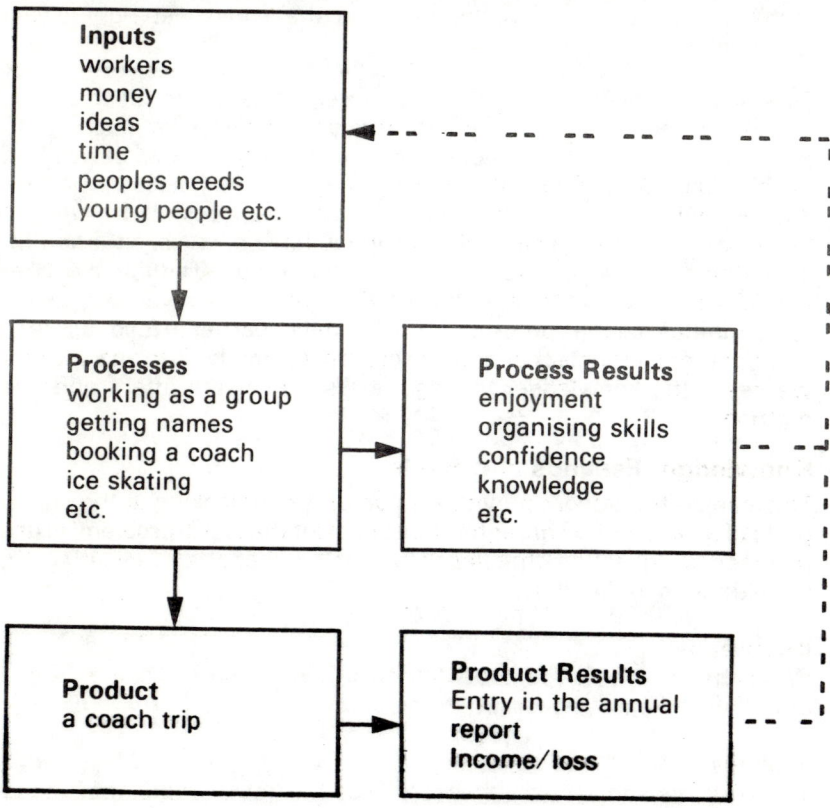

demanded larger deposits and increased the price. Nobody was late for the return journey!

The decision to leave people behind marked an interesting stage in the group's developing confidence and ability to weigh up alternatives. The factors they had taken into consideration included the coach driver's impatience, the responsibility to return younger members home at a reasonable time, the ability of the late four to handle their predicament and the possible strains on friendships (one of the late four was the elder brother of one of the organisers!). Moments of crisis such as this are often one of the few opportunities youth workers have to see if people's feelings and abilities have changed. A difficult decision or action has to be taken and the results lived with. In the event the 'organisers' came out pretty well. They certainly increased in standing within the club and, after some fairly heated exchanges with the four late comers on the next club night, were able to get them to agree that it had been right to leave them behind.

For most of the time the workers were spectators to all this. Their concern, as educators, was with the process results – how much had the trip contributed to the members' ability to do things for themselves? One of the major difficulties with an approach that emphasises process or educational goals is the relative lack of concrete results by which to judge the work. In the case of the trip we have a 'crisis' situation that allows some of the gains to show but it's not the sort of situation workers would like to be in every day of the week. However the lack of opportunities to judge progress is not the major barrier to feedback in the work, rather it is our lack or non use of practical methods to analyse what we see – the knowledge, feelings, skills framework offers one such method.

Knowledge, Feelings and Skills

This simple framework provides a useful way of looking at the various parts of a 'problem'. (Throughout this booklet the word 'problem' is used to mean a "question that faces people" rather than indicating that something is 'difficult'.)

Knowledge
What the person has to know to do the job – what tasks does the job entail, what role is necessary to be successful?

Feelings
The attitudes and values necessary to do the 'job'. For instance, does a particular 'job' mean the person has to tell the truth, remain calm, be cheerful, like people etc? How much confidence does the person require?

Skills
What the person has to be able to do to complete the job. This includes observational/informational skills, thinking skills, communication skills and action skills.

If we view the ice skating trip as a 'problem' to be solved we can see that certain requirements will have to be met:-

The cost and availability of ice skating
Details of coach companies
What the demand is   —   Knowledge
Timing – how long does the journey take
How long do people want on the ice

Figure 2. A framework for knowledge, feelings and skills

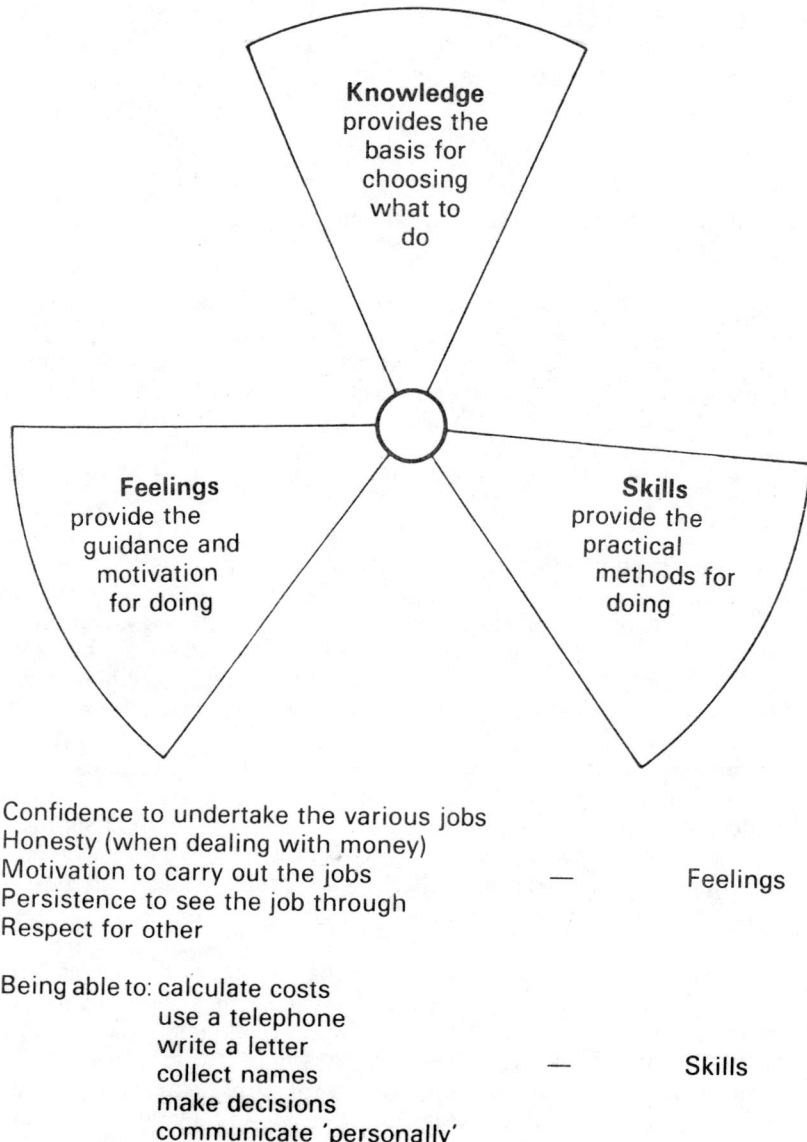

Confidence to undertake the various jobs
Honesty (when dealing with money)
Motivation to carry out the jobs   —   Feelings
Persistence to see the job through
Respect for other

Being able to: calculate costs
　　　　　　 use a telephone
　　　　　　 write a letter
　　　　　　 collect names   —   Skills
　　　　　　 make decisions
　　　　　　 communicate 'personally'

Broken down in this way it is easy to see how young people can flounder when they are told by workers to go away and organise something themselves. A more truly educative approach would involve:

1. **Assessment:** where people are helped to recognise their strengths and weaknesses in relation to organising the trip. This might, for instance, take the form of the worker asking individuals what they feel their strengths and weaknesses are, or a group of young people working it out for themselves. (In the example this process happened informally – Mike, who was a milkman and therefore used to dealing with figures, handled the financial side of the trip. The educational problem here is that someone's 'strength' was being reinforced rather than a 'weakness' counteracted.) It should also be remembered that assessment is not a 'once and for all' event but a continuing process happening in all the stages and modifying people's actions.

2. **Setting objectives:** where the people involved set specific targets for themselves. Frequently objectives emerge fairly easily and obviously during assessment but when they don't, people may need some help in getting their objectives into a form that leads them into action. An example of objective setting is Tony's assessment that he was very unconfident about using the phone to book the coach – it was something he hadn't done before – and his volunteering to do that job.

3. **Learning/doing:** where the necessary knowledge/feelings/skills are gained. To carry on with the example of Tony – he teamed up with Sue who had done much of the organisation of the previous trips and was able to explain to him exactly what he needed to do and say. He then felt able to make the call. (We can see things didn't go smoothly – in his first call to the coach firm he forgot to ask the cost!)

4. **Evaluation:** where people reflect on what has happened and check whether their objectives have been met. In more formal groups this could be an item on the agenda. In the sort of situation described here it could simply involve the worker or another member of the group checking with an individual or the group whether they felt things had gone as they wished.*

Written like this the headings give the impression of airtight compartments when in reality it is a process whose parts greatly overlap. For instance learning takes place in all four 'stages' – often the realisation by an individual (during "assessment") that s/he has a particular strength or weakness is a significant piece of learning. It also appears a far more formal process than it is. All it really does is to put

---

* This four stage approach is similar to that suggested in "Social Skills & Personal Problem Solving – a handbook of methods". (See Further Reading.)

things into a framework that workers (and young people) can internalize so that they have an almost automatic way of analysing things. Organising a skating trip is a fairly major exercise but the everyday tasks around the club, like running the canteen, give workers the chance to use the framework to help people develop abilities without making a big production number of it. A simple example is when a member asks to go on the door – the two minute conversation that follows would benefit from having the knowledge/feelings/skills framework as the basis for making the decision.

The major outcome of such developmental ways of working is not necessarily people's ability to organise a trip or take money on the door but their all round ability to solve problems. 'Knowledge/feelings/skills' and the four stages involved in 'problem solving' are ways of looking at things that young people can latch onto quickly. They can be applied to many of the decisions and situations people have to handle. For this reason it is important that the framework is made an *explicit* part of the work.

Lastly it needs to be remembered that workers are also part of the process – they themselves have strengths and weaknesses that need to be understood and acted upon.

In conclusion

From what has been said so far we can say:-

1. Social education is about process rather than product (creation not consumption).

2. A comprehensive approach to education involves the conscious development of certain knowledge, feelings and skills.

We will go on to look in more detail at how this works in practice and what an appropriate definition of social education might be.

There is a danger when starting small, of under estimating what young people can do. Subsequently Neil did take on more complex tasks – such as organising the lorry for the carnival float – but the process took some time and was deliberately unforced. With other individuals the pace is likely to be different and workers should be far more ready to take risks and force issues. Their ability to do this partly depends on how well they know the individuals concerned – risks need to be calculated. It also depends on the workers' own feelings and skills. There is a need to take chances, to risk failure, not just for the young person's development but also for the workers' own wellbeing. Workers cannot afford to go stale.

The above applies to situations where the individuals concerned have some control, that is, where it is possible to start small. Many of the 'crises' young people experience are not spread over time and don't start small. Events bunch and appear out of sequence but the same principle applies – that is to break issues down into what is usable, to explore the areas where the individual or group does have some understanding and control. A good example of this type of crisis is when young people have to appear in court for the first time. They need to be able to present themselves, understand the procedures and the consequences, handle their feelings and so on. A court appearance is usually seen as a very significant event by the young people concerned. It therefore provides unusually large possibilities for learning if handled properly. The difficulty as far as the worker is concerned is dealing with this sort of 'crisis' is often very time consuming and involves him/her in some difficult choices.

One, largely unintended, consequence of this way of working was that it was a group rather than an individual that organised the trip. So far the focus has been on the development of individual competencies. An approach which also emphasises the development of collective ways of working has significant implications for social education as we will see later.

b. Opportunism

By opportunism I mean that the workers tried to respond to life as it was being experienced rather than, say, laying out a programme which states 'relationships' will be done on such a date, 'contraception' on another. Such a clean developmental approach does not fit well with what actually happens in young people's lives. As already mentioned things often happen all at once rather than being spaced over a period and the "easy crisis" need not appear first. Many workers have discovered that on the whole it is unnecessary to manufacture events or stimuli in order to set people thinking. In fact opportunities for learning exist in such profusion that workers are faced with a major problem of

choice. A key factor here is the workers' ability to recognise and then use the material. This can be illustrated by the following comments from one of the "ice skating workers":-

"I was sat in the office one Tuesday morning when John came in asking to use the phone to fix an appointment with the social security. He didn't know the number so I gave him the phone book. After a couple of minutes he threw the book down, said he couldn't be bothered and left. A week or so later on a club night he wanted to phone up one of the local pubs to finalise a darts team. This time he looked at the phone book, said he couldn't see the number and gave it to me to look up. The number was there alright and I twigged that John couldn't use a phone book".

The worker went on to describe how he had waited for a private moment with John to broach the matter and how he had helped John to construct a small telephone book of his own useful numbers – alphabetically arranged. He still had problems with telephone books (especially the Yellow Pages) but a start had been made.

The fact that the workers were attempting to deal with situations that were felt to be significant by the young people themselves meant that there was the possibility of some 'extraordinary' learning (as in the case of court appearances), but this has to be set against the random and patchy way in which it is taking place. The difficulty with opportunism is that there is a very real danger of throwing the baby out with the bathwater. There is a place in youth work for manufactured stimuli even if it is as simple as putting a newspaper out in the coffee bar or a poster on the wall. Exactly because events often bunch it is not possible to pull out of a particular piece of experience all the various strands at the time, so it will be necessary to try to encourage thought at other times.

Being opportunist is not an excuse for not thinking about or planning the work. For opportunism to be successful workers need to bring to each situation a way of judging what their response should be. 'Knowledge, feelings and skills' is one framework, their personal values and knowledge of the people involved are two others. All this amounts to a considerable "hidden curriculum".

c. Learning by experience

In this approach there is a considerable emphasis on "learning by doing". Most of the problems that face us in our everyday lives can only be solved by us taking action of some kind. We need to be able to deal with officials, make decisions about money, search for information and so on. Yet little has been done in the past in formal education to help people gain the knowledge, feelings and skills necessary to perform these tasks.

Learning by doing (experiential learning) is based on three assumptions, that:

- people learn best when they are personally involved in the learning experience;

- knowledge has to be discovered by the individual if it is to have any significant meaning to them or make a difference in their behaviour; and

- a person's commitment to learning is highest when they are free to set their own learning objectives and are able to actively pursue them within a given framework*

(For a diagramatic view of this process see Figure 3.)

In recent years there has been a growth in teaching social skills, but teachers have faced considerable difficulties because they are dealing with experience at second or third hand. In many respects youth workers

---

* Johnson and Johnson (1974) discuss this process more fully (see further reading).

Figure 3: **Stages in experiential learning**

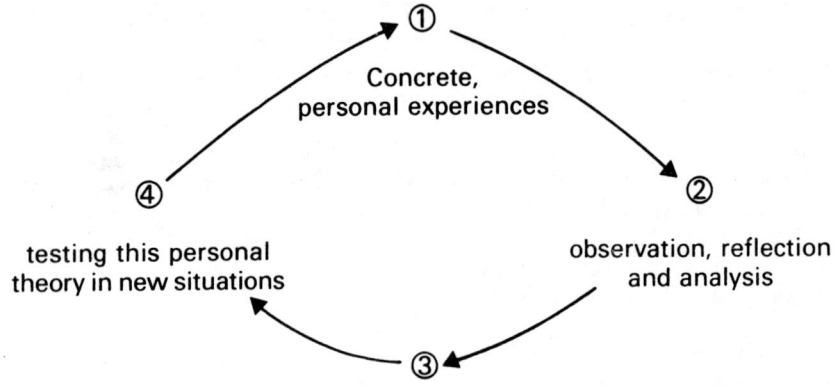

based on Johnson and Johnson page 7.
(See Further Reading.)

have the same difficulty. The workers involved with the ice skating trip were able to use a real event with an outcome (the trip) that definitely mattered not just to the organisers but also to the other twenty or so youngsters who wanted to go skating. The fact that people were engaged in something 'real', rather than say a classroom simulation, is a considerable aid to learning. Here the workers were able to see at first hand what was happening but for much of the time we have to deal with feelings and descriptions of events that we have little immediate or direct knowledge of. Workers are not there when Debbie gets hit by her father or when Stephen is rejected by his mates. Their knowledge is gained vicariously. Social educators therefore have to be sceptical about what is presented as "experience". In a sense their most useful role is to help people identify and understand significant experiences. Yet this is not enough because one of the stranger aspects of adolescence is the way we try to cut ourselves off from certain new experiences.

In adolescence the individual is consciously trying to make sense of the relationship of the external world to him/herself. In doing so s/he is creating a sense of self, of individuality. At this time we are reaching a stage of sexual, intellectual and physical 'readiness', yet we have very little experience of these things to handle this growth. As Richard Sennett has said:

"This is the paradox of adolescence and its terrible unease. So much is possible, yet nothing is happening; lifelong decisions must be made, yet there is little to conceive of it, life in which he is independent, for him to draw on in making up his mind."*

At this moment in their lives young people are experiencing a new and disorderly world. They need to be clear on their relationship to that world so that they might create their own identity. To avoid being painfully overwhelmed there is a tendency to 'invent' or exclude experience to fit their own understanding. This process of assuming the lessons of experience without undergoing the actual experience itself can lead people into holding cruelly sterotyped views and teaches them how to insulate themselves in advance from experiences that seem likely to upset their identity. In other words there is a real danger of people gaining a fixed identity, of them becoming locked in a sort of perpetual adolescence. Workers therefore have to walk on something of a knife edge. On the one hand it is important that young people are not overwhelmed by new and painful experiences, yet on the other if people are to grow and develop they need to actually undergo new experiences. Youth work should not therefore see 'learning by experience' simply as a means, it is also an end – "learning to experience". This is a point we will return to in our later discussion of developmental needs.

d. Being participative

"Participation" has a long and untidy history within youth work. It is an idea much talked about and much misunderstood. The most useful way of approaching the concept is to look at the four main working styles youth workers can adopt.

Telling – which consists if giving straightforward orders often without explanation.

Selling – where the worker has something in mind that s/he wants people to do, such as pony trekking, and then tries to persuade people that it is a good idea and that they should take part.

Participating – is when workers and members jointly make decisions. Thus *both* parties have some control over the final product.

Spectating – in this instance the workers don't intervene in any way – they have no power over what the outcome might be. The members simply get on and do things themselves.

---

* Richard Sennet, The Uses of Disorder, Penguin 1973, p. 27

Figure 4: Youth work styles

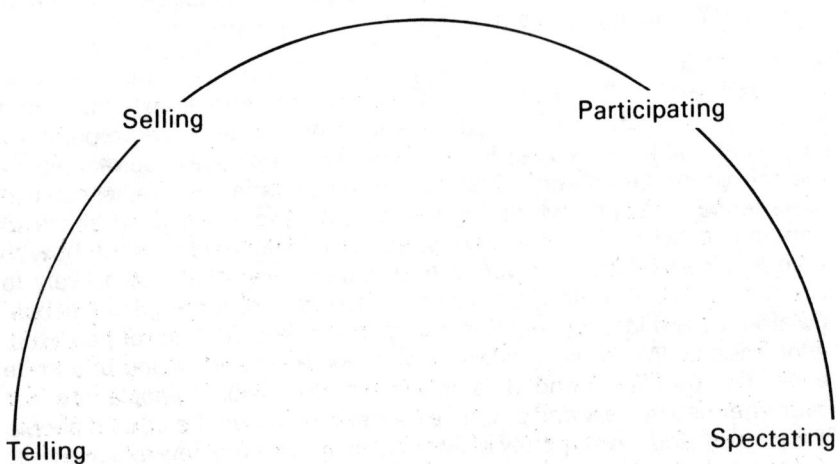

Without a doubt 'selling' is the most common approach in youth work. Just as advertisers and marketing people have become more subtle in their selling over the years – so have youth workers. Instead of simply putting a notice up advertising a football team we might now engage in market research – surveying opinions and then promoting the most popular product. Selling in this form can often pass as participation but the significant difference lies in the fact that ultimately it is the workers who have the power – it is they who in the end define the product – the club's "programme". The only power the members have in this example is to 'vote with their feet' – they can take it or leave it.

Obviously each of these approaches shades into another and it is often difficult to place a particular piece of work precisely. However the framework can show a general direction. Within a club different pieces of the work can fall within different approaches. For instance members usually have little say in who the leaders are – they are told or sold a particular group of people. On the other hand they might have a considerable role in the making of the club's programme. It is therefore important to clearly define the areas under discussion.

Here "participation" is being presented as one of a number of different *means* a worker uses in his/her work. A common mistake made in youth work is to see participation as an end in itself. In some reports and pieces of writing the word seems to have gained an almost magical status. The significance of "participation" is in how it can help social education. For instance we have already discussed the need for young people to have certain new experiences so as to develop. One thing a participative style does is to value their contributions and thoughts and this is a new experience for many young people.

Three major and inter-related sets of reasons are given by workers as to why a participative way of working is appropriate to youth work:-

1. **It matches their personal values and attitudes.** In general participation reflects an optimistic view of the world, whilst a reliance on strict hierarchial structures tends to show a pessimistic view of human nature. One of youth work's main values (as we will see later) is the belief that there is good in everyone.
2. **It makes sound management sense.** Youth groups, because they are heavily dependent on the voluntary effort of both adults and young people, should have a method of management that recognises the special status and needs involved. When people feel, and are, involved in the making of decisions they are more likely to carry the decisions out.
3. **It makes good educational sense.** For reasons already discussed, a participative style allows increased motivation and communication and the learning involved in working in groups.

There would seem to be seven main requirements for a participative style of youth work.

1. **Decisions should be taken by the appropriate people.** This is made possible by having clear decision making structures that follow the principle of taking decisions where they hurt. That is to say the decision is taken by the people it will affect most. These structures should be adhered to.

2. **Decisions should be taken in groups.** participation is a communal experience, it is not simply making sure that everyone is consulted. Participation is about encouraging people to act and think collectively, to co-operate, and to feel part of a group. This is not to say that every single decision needs to be taken in a group but that decisions need to be taken with reference to a group. All this has implications for the size of groups. Whether the club has 30 or 150 members, on the whole they will have roughly the same number of committed and active members who share in the organisation and running of the group. Splitting the group and improving staffing ratios are only limited solutions. A participative style, if it is to be successful, therefore, involves the use of reasonably small units.

3. **The decision must be real.** The issues should be significant and the decision acted upon. One of the most common criticisms made of 'participation' in youth work is that the matters covered are trivial and that outcomes are conveniently forgotten if they are not to the worker's taste.

4. **Decision makers should be accountable for their actions.** Two points need noting here. First, people should not on the whole be shielded from the consequences of their decisions. Where unpleasantness or difficulties result from a decision made by a group of young people, it is not uncommon for workers to step in to 'protect the youngsters'. This rather cuts across the educational nature of the experience. People have to learn that participation also involves taking responsibility for your actions. Second, where participation involves the use of small groups, it is crucial that some mechanism is adopted that keeps the group or committee in close touch with what the wider membership thinks. Furthermore, such groups should be accountable to the wider membership for their actions*.

5. **The decision makers must have the knowledge, feelings and skills necessary.** Thus they must have adequate information, the ability to work together as a group, confidence and so on.

6. **A youth work style should be adopted that enables people to have the appropriate opportunities, resources and abilities.** So far there have been a number of things suggested for this – a concern for process, starting small and using learning by doing. Further suggestions are made about workers' values and attitudes and the need to put the work in its social and political context.

7. **Participation needs time.** It takes time for people to develop skills (and to realise that they have developed them!). Time is important on two counts. First it is usually necessary for a group to exist over a period of time for the necessary feelings and attitudes to grow. Second workers need to devote substantial time to such projects.

The ice skating workers were fairly strong on the last six requirements but weak on the first. The structures in which the young people were operating were not that clear or appropriate. The club did have a members' committee which included several of the people involved in organising the trip to the ice rink in London. Yet the decision to organise the trip was taken on the spur of the moment by the workers and members that happened to troup into the office with Neil that club night. There was no question that the committee would have approved the trip especially as several of its leading lights were involved but that sort of instantaneous by-passing is bound to undermine it. Herein lies a tension which has to be resolved – between the desire of the workers to be able to respond quickly and the need for consistency and fairly rational decision making. Another course in this instance might have been to encourage Neil to get a list of names and to present a case at the next members' committee.

---

* For guidelines about working and making decisions in small groups see section 1 of **Organise!** (details in Further Reading).

In this particular example the workers were also not as strong as they might have been on the second requirement – that decisions should be made in groups. As we have seen the decision to go ice skating just happened – it involved a number of people – but were they a group? The first decision, to gauge the members' response, was taken by the workers and Neil. The second, to book dates, the rink and the coach, was taken by a number of members including some of the members committee. The next decision about cost and financial arrangements was taken by three members of the committee – Mike, Sue and Tony. Such a mish mash worked and was acceptable because there was a history of participation in the club and because the process was progressive ie in the end it was the people who had responsibility for finance who actually took decisions about money and costs. The people involved did feel a part of a group – they were all fairly central members of the club. However, had there been any problems or disagreements at this stage then the fragile nature of this sort of ad-hoc approach would have been shown.

There is a real danger in this sort of situation of the worker getting drawn into taking on what seem attractive roles for him/herself and so denying young people access to learning. One of the most difficult times for workers using this approach is when things appear to be going wrong. Does the worker stride in and save the day or does s/he remain in an enabling role even if it means the thing the members are organising fails? In some cases the experience of failure may do more harm than good, in others it can be a valuable experience. The only general rules here is that the young people concerned must agree to the worker taking on a different role (like selling or telling) and that any action taken must help meet peoples' developmental needs.

e. The social context

One of the topics the workers often talked over was the extent to which their work was about containing ideas and behaviour that the rest of society found undesireable. These conversations were often sparked off by remarks about the character of the club's membership. A good number of the members were in some sort of touble with the law or were what the social workers called "at risk". The youth office had an ambivalent view of these young people. On the one hand they frequently justified their share of the resource cake by claiming that money spent on the youth service stopped vandalism and anti-social behaviour but on the other they complained about the bad name such young people gave the club. The idea that youth work was simply about curbing vandalism and so called anti-social behaviour disturbed the workers. There was no doubt that the workers wanted to encourage changes in young people's attitudes and behaviour. They were concerned about the unhappiness and pain that 'trouble' both reflected and caused but they tried to link the troubles with broader issues.

Making links is important. Many personal troubles simply cannot be dealt with by the individual or their immediate family or friends because they are linked with public issues.* An illustration of the realtionship between personal troubles and public issues is the housing situation currently facing young people. A young woman or man who wants, but cannot find, suitable accommodation has a personal trouble. On the other hand the lack of adequate housing is a public issue. When a worker helps to find someone accommodation s/he is tackling a personal trouble only. Currently there is less adequate accommodation for single people than people wanting it, thus only a limited number of personal troubles can be solved. Consequently workers, if they want to help in alleviating all personal housing problems they must also work with young people on the public issue – the expansion of local housing for single people. By setting the personal in its social and political context and, for instance, recognising that housing is a political problem, these workers were taking an important step. They were no longer suggesting that it was the young persons 'fault' that they could not get accommodation.

The nineteenth century philosophical origins of youth work have, over the years, given strength to the view that individuals are to blame for their misfortunes. It was people's own fault, for instance, that they were poor or ill. What was wrong was people's inability to save, rather than the economic system which gave them low wages. Youth workers therefore needed to instil the relevant virtues such as thrift and self discipline in their young charges. By being careful and working hard poverty could be avoided. This lack of sociological understanding was mirrored in the sixties and early seventies where youth workers adopted the group work methods of writers like Carl Rogers. Here again was the concentration on the individual and his/her immediate group which led to an overemphasis on psychological factors and an ignoring of the social context of the work. Such analysis, whilst perhaps helping people in one direction, may have disabled them in others.

The skating workers were keen to make connections, to understand private troubles within their economic/political setting. One of the main links they made in this respect was with class. Most of the club's members came from two adjacent council estates and their values, attitudes and way of life could only be described as working class. One of the most common feelings amongst young working class men and

---

* C Wright Mills talks about this relationship in The Sociological Imagination, Penguin, 1970, p 14–16

women is their sense of powerlessness in the face of the major economic and politcal processes that govern their lives. To be told that it is their 'fault' that they are unemployed or can't get housing, for instance, is to further compound that sense of resignation and powerlessness. This is the importance of making connections – not only does a better understanding lead to the possibility of more realistic action – but it liberates people from the burden of unnecessary guilt. It suggests that the most useful role a worker can adopt is to separate the "problem" from the person. Because a problem affects a particular individual or group it does not mean it is of their making. And because a problem is not wholly of their making it can only be solved when consideration is given to all the major factors involved. This is the challenge facing youth workers – to recognise that many personal troubles cannot be solved merely as troubles, but can only be fully understood in terms of public issues.

In conclusion

In this chapter I have looked more closely at five elements of the way the ice skating workers operated. They:

a. tried to break down complex events into usable pieces;
b. used existing opportunities rather than created them;
c. used "learning by experience";
d. were participative; and
e. put their work in its social context.

This group of workers were only able to work in this way because they had a shared and common set of aims and objectives and they knew what each other were doing. In other words, they were a team. For these workers at this stage, the sense of common purpose had come about more by luck than judgement. They were friends, had similar backgrounds and interests, and met socially. They often talked about the club and its members. However, they were very unsystematic in the way they did these things and a few months after the trip, when some pretty basic decisions had to be made about the future of the club, the need for a more formal and systematic approach to the staff team became apparent. For this sort of approach to be successfully applied we must therefore add a sixth element – the need to create and maintain a team approach to youth work.

3. Rediscovering social education

So far we have been looking at a form of youth work that puts learning first. In this chapter I want to ask what makes this form of learning special enough to have its own label – social education?

Our starting point will be a discussion of the major reasons for wanting to 'socially educate' people and the forming of the following definition:-

> Social education is the conscious attempt to help people to gain for themselves, the knowledge, feelings and skills necessary to meet their own and others developmental needs.

We will then go on to examine some of the value issues involved in social education and, in Chapter 4, the political implications of this view.

Developmental needs

The view of social education advocated here is initially based on two beliefs:

1. All members of society have the right to a full emotional, social and intellectual development.

2. Society has an obligation to ensure that people get access to the resources and opportunities that enable such development.

One way of looking at what these developmental needs are has been put forward by Mia Kellmer Pringle (see figure 5). She suggests that there are four significant developmental needs:-

a. The need for love and security
b. The need for new experiences
c. The need for praise and recognition
d. The need for responsibility*

These needs are met in a variety of ways – by the family unit, school, work, friends etc. In this sense, social education is not just the property of youth work. The relative importance of each of these areas varies through time and with age. For instance, certain needs will be more important in adolescence than in early childhood. During adolescence (which I take to mean the period from puberty to about the age of maturity – in other words from around age 11 to about 18 years) a number of significant things are happening. Young men and women are having to:

- come to terms with new and sometimes worrying physical experiences such as the boy's first 'wet dream' or the girl's first period.
- explore their sexual identity
- answer questions concerning job choice and employment/unemployment
- change their relationships with parents, friends, adults
- develop a self concept/identity.

Looking at this list of 'new experiences' there is a danger of getting a rather melodramatic view of adolescence. Most young people are able to get through this period without great 'storm and stress'. This is not to say that they will not experience difficulties or do not need help, but simply a plea to keep things in perspective. Nor should we forget the significance of adolescence and other critical periods of transition. In recent years it has become increasingly clear that the experiences of adolescence rate in equal importance with those of the first five years of life in their effect on what happens in later life.†

---

* Mia Kellmer Pringle, The Needs of Children, Hutchinson, 1980
   I've chosen to use this framework as it presents developmental needs as being interrelated and interdependent. Other formulations such as 'Maslows Triangle' suggest that such needs operate in a hierarchical sequence. The most basic needs are for sheer survival (like the needs for food, water and shelter). Only when these have been met do other needs emerge (like the need for a loving relationship). There is now a great deal of evidence to show that things do not operate is such a smooth way.

† John Coleman gives a good summary of the evidence here (see Further Reading).

Figure 5: **Developmental Needs**
Mia Kellmer Pringle has suggested that there are four significant developmental needs which have to be met from birth. These are:

a. **The need for love and security**
   This is probably the most important need as it provides the basis for all later relationships. On it depends the development of the personality – the ability to care and respond to affection. A continuous, reliable, loving relationship first within the family unit, then with a growing number of others can meet this need. It can give the individual a sense of worthwhileness and of a coherent personal identity.

b. **The need for new experiences**
   New experiences are a fundamental requirement for mental growth. In early life it is largely through play and language that the child explores the world and learns to cope with it. In adolescence another form of play is important – this time the experiments with different kinds of role – girlfriend/boyfriend/worker/leader. Language remains a crucial factor in intellectual growth – it helps in learning to reason, to think and in making relationships.

c. **The need for praise and recognition**
   Growing up requires a tremendous amount of learning – emotional, social and intellectual. Consequently strong incentives are necessary for the individual to continue through the difficulties and conflicts s/he will inevitably encounter. The most effective incentives are praise and recognition sustained over time.

d. **The need for responsibility**
   This need is met by allowing the child to gain personal independence, firstly through learning to look after him/herself in matters of everyday care and then through a gradual extension of responsibility over other areas until s/he has the freedom and ability to decide on his/her own actions and, indeed, to be able to accept responsibility for others.

Adapted from Mia Kellmer Pringle, The Needs of Children, 1980

If we examine these developmental needs we can see that the skating trip workers were working in all four areas. In their relationship with Neil, (the instigator of the trip), they were particularly concerned with his self centredness and apparent inability to take responsibility for his own actions. Over a lengthy period they had tried to show he mattered to them and as the relationship began to be reciprocated, (albeit in occasionally peculiar ways), their concern shifted. They encouraged him to take on new roles – such as that of 'organiser' and they tried to reinforce his behaviour in these roles with encouragement and support. In the case of the trip we see them seeking to get his acceptance of a degree of responsibility for others.

The majority of young people these workers were dealing with could not be considered as having such profound difficulties in making and keeping relationships. They at least had a relatively secure personality base from which they could handle new experiences. These young people were beginning to take responsibility for their own lives and were seeking an identity and view of the world that was of their own making. Decisions, for instance about sex, were being taken that could no longer be discussed in the family. They therefore desired a more independent and equal relationship with adults than that found at school or home. The workers saw these needs for 'autonomy', for responsibility and new experiences, as being the primary areas for their attention. However this didn't stop them from trying to meet other needs as they were recognised.

When youth workers' efforts are put into the total context of young people's lives it quickly becomes apparent that there is the need for some humility about how much they can achieve. As we have seen young people are having to handle experiences and take on new roles that many find difficult to talk and think about in the family or at school. They often need the help of sympathetic outsiders (like youth workers), but the family (in particular) and the school are still very powerful forces in determining young peoples' life chances and attitudes. However the ice skating workers demonstrate that youth workers can have a unique and special role. The intervention of youth workers can be significant in many young peoples' lives and crucial in some.

The use of developmental needs has three further important implications for social education. Firstly, whilst earlier approaches to social education have usually centred on the idea of adults helping young people, a developmental needs approach doesn't make that assumption. It recognises that adults also have social educational needs and that these can be met by young people. In addition it takes into account of the help young people give each other, for instance the caring and security they get through friendships. This whole area of mutual aid is crying out for youth workers' attention. The tendency has been to concentrate on direct intervention with the person who has the 'problem' rather than to work through intermediaries. For instance when a young person has to appear in court for the first time the worker might sit down with the person concerned and run through what an appearance involves. How much better would be an approach that gave another young person who had actually had the same experience and who uses the same language, the knowledge, feelings and skills to be able to answer questions and give support. Not only do you answer the first person's need but you also extend another person's competence in the process.

Secondly, a developmental needs approach, like other ways of looking at social education, places a special emphasis on groups. These needs are largely met through interaction with others and the experience of being a member of a group. Groups are essential parts of human existence. They provide us with both a sense of belonging and the experience necessary for the creation of our own separate identity. It is also necessary to work collectively in order to influence the political system so that all developmental needs be met.

Thirdly, the employment of developmental needs neatly side-steps the definitional problems involved with the concept of 'maturity'. The achievement of this state has usually been the central aim of previous approaches. By adopting developmental needs we are saying that our central concern is personal growth rather than the attainment of the magical status of being a 'mature person'. In other words we are defining maturity as the search for maturity.

If the meeting of developmental needs is seen as a 'problem' then certain knowledge, feelings and skills will be necessary to fulfil them. Added to the comments made above we can move towards a definition of social education as follows:-

"Social education is the conscious attempt to help people to gain for themselves, the knowledge, feelings and skills necessary to meet their own and others developmental needs."

To sum up, this definition has substantial advantages over previous formulations. It is:-

1. **Unambiguous** – it avoids the lack of clarity engendered by the use of words like maturity.

2. **More dynamic** – the concept of developmental needs and the knowledge, feelings, skills framework provide prescriptions for action.

3. **All embracing** – social education is not seen as the property of youth work but of several major institutions – schools, the family, friends etc.

4. **Conscious** – people often confuse social **learning** with social **education**. Education is a deliberate attempt to change people. Learning is what is gained from that process and from all social situations (intended or not).

Values

Education is about conscious change. It is about trying to alter people in some way. The direction which it takes, the changes in people that workers see as desirable, depend on the values we bring to the work. Value questions run through all that youth workers do, yet they are rarely talked about in any detail. One of the major reasons for this is the inconsistencies that often emerge between our personal values and our practice. It is altogether more comfortable not to question what we are doing. Another reason for our reluctance, is that we are often apprehensive about admitting that youth work is an attempt to change people in a **particular** way. Workers who are connected with movements that have strong ideas about what is right and wrong, such as those involved with church groups, tend to be most clear about this. We all have ideas about the sort of behaviour and feelings that are desirable and these ideas rightly and inevitably influence the way we work with young people even if we are not entirely conscious of the fact. The first step any educator must take is to be clear about these values. Clarity is important, firstly, because clear aims lead to more effective action and secondly because the people you are working with have the right to know what you are trying to do with them.

In what has been written so far it is possible to see nine broad ideas that might qualify as values. These ideas would seem to have an intrinsic worth and are about the way workers should operate. To a certain extent these 'doing' or 'instrumental' values are also some of the very qualities social educators want to encourage in the people they are working with.

1. **Problems should be defined by the person who "owns" them.**
The problems should be self-defined – it is not up to the worker to say what the problem is but for the person/persons to work it out for themselves. People will be more motivated to solve a problem they have defined rather than what the worker has said they should do.

From the cover of the 1st Edition of Creators Not Consumers

This is sometimes known as peoples 'right to self determination'.

2. **Seeing the good in everyone.** We need to accept people as they are and not as what they could become. It is essential to be optimistic about people's potential so as not to limit their growth. In other words we must try to like and respect the people we work with.

3. **Honesty.** Explicitness is important, that is people need to understand exactly what is happening. More broadly openness is also valued. Work should be carried out in a spirit of 'straightforwardness', not having something 'up your sleeve'. A part of this is the need to be oneself and to be able to talk about your own feelings etc.

4. **Consistency.** Workers should deal with young people evenly. They need to do this in order that they gain people's trust. Consistency also implies management, that workers are clear about their aims, methods of working and evaluation, that is they need to be disciplined in their approach.

5. **Flexibility.** Whilst being consistent, workers also need to be flexible, as different people and situations need different responses. This implies that the worker should not start from a narrow ideological base but have a choice of theories and practice at his/her disposal.

6. **Common Sense.** This is a belief that reason should be applied to all situations, that whilst feelings are very important, it is important to try and look on those feelings "objectively".

7. **Freedom of Choice.** Whilst it is the responsibility of the workers to offer help, people must be free to choose whether they take up the offer. The offer itself must enhance the individual or group's freedom to choose.

8. **Equality.** The desired relationship between the workers and the young people is two way, mutual, not leader/led. Both workers and young people have needs to be satisfied. The problems/needs which are at the centre of youth work are 'owned' by young people and are for them to define. The worker's role is to help people to better understand and take action on needs and possible solutions and that role can only be on an equal footing.

9. **Confidentiality.** Ownership of problems must be respected. What the worker hears about problems should be treated as confidential and passed onto others only if permission is given.

This list of values shows up some of the ethical problems that workers experience. It shows how difficult it is for a worker to be morally neutral (even if that is desirable). Even the very act of intervening in peoples lives is based on certain value assumptions:

- people should not passively accept their conditions but actively intervene to change them.
- people should plan ahead.

Workers would be less than human of their values did not show through in their work. For instance if the worker is counselling a pregnant young woman who is very unsure about having an abortion, it is likely they themselves would favour one decision or course of action. The way questions are phrased, the information provided and the tone of the conversation are bound to influence the person in some way. To this must be added the fact that people frequently expect workers to be moral agents.

Lastly there is a question about how absolute these values are. Is it always right to keep confidences? Are there times when a worker should lie? Should workers respect a young persons determination to be dishonest or irrational?

We can see here the makings of a real contradiction – if, as educators, we are trying to alter people in some way, does this not place limits on their right to self determination?

Such tensions are an inevitable part of working with people. To some extent the dilemmas can be eased by workers:

1. Knowing their own values. When workers are clear about their own values they are more likely to be aware of their own attempts to smuggle those values into their work.

2. Being open about their own values. By being open the worker lets other people know where they stand and they can then act accordingly.

3. Ensuring that any action they take actually enhances peoples' freedom of choice. Workers should enable people to have experiences that gives them the knowledge, feelings and skills necessary for them to be able to make choices and so make real their values.*

---

* Value dilemmas such as those discussed in Allen Pincus and Anne Minahan, Social Work Practice: Model and Method, Peacock, 1973.

As these conclusions make clear there are no simple solutions to value problems in social education. Each situation has to be judged on its own merits. However, what this discussion does indicate is that an awareness of such ethical considerations must become a part of the basic beliefs of social education.

In conclusion

This chapter has put forward the idea that social education is the conscious attempt to help people to gain for themselves the knowledge, feelings and skills necessary to meet their own and others developmental needs. It has suggested that:

1. All members of society have the right to a full emotional, social and intellectual development.

2. Society has an obligation to ensure that people gain access to the resources and opportunities that enable such development.

3. The help given to people must be based on truth and reason and enhance human freedom and dignity.

In the next chapter we will see that such a full development can only be achieved and maintained by action at both an individual and a collective level.

4. Social education and politics

Whilst many of the young people we work with face incredible injustices, are ignorant of their rights and are racist and sexist, our normal reaction is that these are areas that somehow, someone else should do something about. In this chapter I want to say why this will just not do. I want to show why youth workers, if they are to be honest in what they do, must turn away from surface polishing and grapple with the problems of politics and power.

The politics of developmental needs

Issues like racism or powerlessness are so big that it is difficult to see what we can do about them. The very word 'politics' is enough to strike horror into the hearts of managers and bring boredom to the faces of young people. Yet we can't escape its consequences. The problem we have to face is that by ignoring politics in our day to day youth work we may actually be restricting people's ability to meet their developmental needs.

Perhaps the best way into this problem is to look back at those developmental needs. The need that shows the problem at its clearest is the fourth – the need for responsibility. People cannot take responsibility for their own lives in a vacuum. We live in society and our actions must, therefore, affect others. Thus when the young organisers of the trip gained the space and resources to carry through their idea, these had to be largely won at someone else's 'expense'.

In other words, there had been a shift of power.

> **Power:** The capacity of an individual or group to make and carry out decisions and, more broadly, to determine what goes on the decision making agenda. Such decisions may be made against the interests and/or opposition of others.

Power in our society is very unevenly distributed. The young people we work with have only a slim chance of ever having any real control over the events and institutions that shape their lives. Looking back at the value base of social education we took two basic beliefs as our starting point:-

1. All members of society have a right to a full emotional, social and intellectual development.
2. Society has an obligation to ensure that people get access to the resources and opportunities that enable such development.

Whilst workers may believe society has an obligation to all its members, in reality that obligation is far from being fully honoured. A privileged few take a disproportionately large share of the resources and opportunities. This places social educators in a real dilemma. As soon as they try to enable a growth in people's power to make and carry through decisions they are challenging the distribution of power and, therefore, acting politically.* Conversely, when workers ignore or avoid this political dimension they are, in effect, limiting people's social development and so maintaining the power structure. Thus in an unjust society, where power is in the hands of the few, social educators can never be neutral or 'non-political'.

The significance of this point cannot be overemphasised. Within these values and within social education generally there is a tension between the interests of individuals and groups. The decisions an individual takes about his/her life must affect others. The way in which this restriction works is determined by the values society acts upon. We therefore need rules that ensure people keep their rights and don't infringe upon others'. Just such a set of rules is provided by the instrumental or 'doing' values we discussed in the last chapter. They can be translated into political values such as

- **a belief in human freedom,** i.e. the opportunity to make significant choices in a self willed and uncoerced way:

---

* As I understand it politics is to do with power in society, (whether that society be a tribe, a nation state or some other type); the relations between societies; and the social movements, organisations and institutions which are directly involved in the determination of such power.

- **justice** or what is a fair way to make social decisions; and
- **equality,** the impartial treatment of people, where discrimination is based only on the recognition of just and relevant differences.

Ultimately it is only in a society within which people act upon such principles that everybody's developmental needs can be adequately met and safeguarded. Unfortunately, we do not live as yet in such a society and this has important implications for social education. To begin to understand these implications we must return to our definition.

> Social education is the conscious attempt to help people to gain for themselves, the knowledge, feelings and skills necessary to meet their own and others' developmental needs.

If we follow the logic of our definition through then the 'necessary knowledge, feelings and skills' mentioned must also include those of politics. So it is that social education is not just political but has to be **consciously** political. It has to be a practice that actively helps people to gain the necessary knowledge, feelings and skills to think and act politically (i.e. political education). The question becomes not whether or not social education is political, but given that it is **political** what should workers do?

What should workers do?
Firstly workers need to clarify and be open about their values.
Discussions about values are not very common in youth work. Rarer still is any consistent attempt to test our actions against our values. One of the main arguments of this book is that values need to play a more central role in youth work. First, clearer aims lead to more effective action. Second, as social education cannot be neutral we must be open about what we are doing. The people educators work with have a right to know what is being done with them. This last point is a particularly sensitive one where politics is concerned. There is much talk in political education of 'bias' and 'indoctrination'. As values are such a central part of human experience bias is inevitable and important. Our values are our 'bias'. They are our humanness. Do we want or even need 'balance'? It is frequently people's 'bias' that touches us most. We do not adopt values through pure reasoning, (indeed there is a sense in which our values are beyond reason), but because we *feel* that they are right. This feeling often comes about because we have known someone who passionately believes in a certain value and tries to live his/her life by it. Anyway who wants to be 'balanced' about justice or freedom or equality? These are values which social educators, quite frankly, should be trying to convince people of. All that youth workers have to remember is that they

are educators and are therefore bound by education's values of openness and explicitness.

There are many different ways in which workers can clarify their values and understand their political meaning. It is very much a case of choosing a method that speaks to a workers condition. However, one point that does need emphasising is that within social education, value clarification should be both an individual and a group exercise. We have already suggested the need to build upon a teamwork approach. For that approach to have any success it is essential that there is agreement and compatability about the ends you want to achieve and means used to get there. It therefore follows that workers need to explore together (and with young people), the values on which they base their practice.*

A further important step is for workers to examine what their values may mean in the lives of the people they work with. Choosing values is an intensely personal affair. By and large it is not the worker who has to live with the consequences of his/her intervention in another person's life. For this reason much importance has been placed on the idea that problems should be defined by the person who 'owns' them. The values we, as workers, hold can be experienced and understood in a completely different way by others. What we may see as sensible 'rules' about behaviour (such as the 'doing' values already discussed) can be experienced as oppressive by the people they are applied to. Workers therefore need to be constantly checking the appropriateness of what they are encouraging.

Second, workers need to understand how concentrating on individual needs maintains the power structure.
Workers will have to recognise that the concentration on the needs of the individual and small group that has characterised social education up until now may actually work to maintain the uneven distribution of power and so negate their efforts. This may appear to be a harsh judgement to many but an examination of the way power is maintained within our society shows why this may be so.

When people have power, they, not unnaturally, want to hold on to it. In simple terms this involves the creation of two groups, one on top of the other, using a process known as subordination. The top, powerful group maintains its distinctiveness from the larger, bottom group by setting certain entry requirements. In our society it could be argued that the two main requirements are the possession of:
- property; and/or
- academic or professional qualifications.

---

* For some suggestions about how workers can personally explore the issues raised in this chapter see Further Reading.

Today it is more difficult than in the past for members of the top or dominant group to pass on their privileged status to their sons and daughters. Their children do, of course, start with a special advantage. There is likely to be a background of academic or other success, an environment which encourages the gaining of qualifications and money for special schooling and help. The result is that children in middle class families stand a much greater chance of academic success (e.g. over 70% of students attending polytechnics and universities are from middle class families). Also while rising death duties may have made the passing on of the advantages of wealth more difficult, a similar 'improvement' in tax avoidance has meant that little difference has been made.

Members of the bottom or excluded group are faced with two choices if they want to increase their power. The first *individualistic* response is to attempt to get the necessary qualifications/property that will gain them entry. As we have seen, members of the top group have a head start here. They can also alter the entry requirements if it looks like too many people from the bottom group are getting in.

An alternative choice is the *collective* achievement of power. Here members of the excluded group join and work together in order to take power for the benefit of the group as a whole. Examples of this sort of action would be the day to day conflicts between trade unions and employers, the efforts of ethnic and racial groups to attain civil rights and the attempts of womens groups and organisations to achieve full equality with men. The excluded group's main strength is its ability to mobilise significant numbers of people in such things as strikes, pickets, demonstrations, marches and so on. As such, collective responses often find themselves with legal problems (not unexpectedly as the power holders use the legal system to maintain their own position). The types of action already mentioned can also be very costly in personal terms and are therefore difficult to sustain over a long period.

To sum up, the top or dominant group is in a strong position to hold on to power. It makes the rules (and therefore has 'the law' on its side), its sons and daughters have a head start in gaining the necessary entry requirements and its methods of getting and keeping power involve fewer direct personal costs. When we look at what youth workers do, the significance of this analysis quickly shows itself.

Social educators only work with a small proportion of the youth population. As long as they continue to emphasise individual needs to the exclusion of collective needs, all they will be doing is to oil the wheels of the subordination process. An example of this sort of process is when workers help young people to get jobs by tackling things like self-presentation and social skills. They are dealing with a private trouble yet the public issue is a considerable shortfall of jobs. The collective or public need is for an expansion of job opportunities or their alternative. If the worker is successful s/he merely alters which individuals get through the gate into the privileged group. The worker does not affect the overall balance between the groups. In other words, s/he meets the needs of one group at the expense of the other.

Here then, is the challenge facing social educators. They have traditionally worked in individualistic areas, 'private troubles'. By doing so, they have contributed toward the smoother functioning of a system that their values would appear to be in conflict with. If they are to bring their practice into line with their values then they have to work in the area of collective action. They must deal with 'public issues'.

Third, workers need to understand the relation of young people to power.
We often talk about young people's 'powerlessness' without fully grasping the nature of their position. As well as being young, young people also have a particular gender, race and class and through these will experience power in different ways.

If we begin at a general level we can see that *individually* young people have not accumulated significant property or qualification. In addition they are not in a position to take sustained collective action. The institutions to which they belong (such as schools) discourage it; they have, as yet, little of the knowledge, feelings or skills necessary for successful actions; and the whole period is one of change which works against any sustained activity. Where they join community organisations such as political parties and unions, their interests and actions are frequently seen as an irritant, something those organisations could do without.

The one major power young people have is a *negative* one – their ability to be a threat to order. It was such a fear of the mob which fanned the development of youth work in the late nineteenth century and it is a similar fear which has more recently loosened municipal purse strings in a number of metropolitan areas. It is, however, a difficult power for young people to take any advantage of.

Beyond this general level there are big differences in the way young people experience power. We should not isolate the mechanisms we have been discussing from the classes they create. To a large extent, young people's experience of power will be affected by the relationship of their families to the subordination process. Thus children from families in the dominant group are likely to gain certain ideas, feelings and skills – those which reinforce the 'rightness' of their position and their ability to hold on to it. In a similar way young people who come from families where there has been a history of involvement in collective action will be affected by that experience. Their view of the nature of power and how it is achieved will generally be different from the children of the 'top' group, but they also could be prepared to act politically. Young people from families who have suffered subordination without taking collective action are unlikely to possess such confidence, knowledge or skills. They also have a more restricted access to the means to take action.

If the young person's class position and familiarity with political action is important then their *potential* class position is also significant. In advance of their fulfilling the full entry requirements for membership of the dominant group, young people who look like getting a good range of academic/professional qualifications or achieving a substantial holding of property can often be allowed to develop and exercise power 'on licence'. A classic example of this process is the government patronage of student unions.

Beyond class and age two further characteristics need careful attention – gender and race. They remain deep and powerful means of discrimination.

Firstly, at an *individualistic* level there is a great deal of evidence about the under-representation of women and minority ethnic groups in higher education, apprenticeships, and training for the 'professions'.

They are, therefore, falling down on the 'qualification' entry to the dominant group. Secondly, in relation to *collective action* we can see that women and members of minority ethnic groups do not occupy such a strategic position in the labour market. The sectors of the labour force that have industrial 'muscle' such as the power workers are predominantly white and male. Women tend to occupy low paid and part-time jobs spurned by men which are, almost by definition, weak in industrial power. Similarly, Black and Asian workers tend to be in the low paid sector.

Members of minority ethnic groups, then, face a double exclusion. They are usually members of the subordinate class and, therefore, experience the dominant class's attempts to keep them from getting too powerful. However they also experience racism from white members of both classes. Thus, for instance, ethnic minorities are harder hit by unemployment, do not achieve formal positions of power and fail to have their interests adequately represented by trade unions. A similar argument can be made about women's experience.

To fully understand the experience of young people we must use ideas such as class, gender and race. Rather too often in the past we have used the category 'youth' in a far too general way and so ignored the profound differences in experience that, for instance, class generates. Such differences also find expression in the way we, as youth workers, operate.

Fourth, we need to recognise that these society wide processes are reproduced in our work.
This process of subordination is reproduced in the way youth workers and groups work. If we take any of the four concepts previously discussed – class, age, gender and race – and apply them to our day to day youth work then the reproduction becomes clear. A useful example is class.

From what research evidence we have it can be seen that there is a high proportion of middle class young people involved in youth club committees. The same can be said of other forms of youth participation such as school councils, local youth councils, and in self programming groups such as the Young Farmers. We should not be surprised at this, as these young people are the 'sons and daughters' of the middle class sponsors of such attempts at participation. They know how to behave, feel they have a *right* to participate and are confident that they have something worth saying. Also they have access to the right sort of knowledge and opportunities. Interestingly the one club members committee in the main piece of research in this area that had a substantial working class membership was based in a coal mining area where there was a strong history of collective (trade union) action.* If we look at the example we started with, the 'skating trip' club, a high proportion of its active membership either had parents that were heavily involved in working class organisations such as trade unions and social clubs or were middle class. These examples underline the importance of family or community experience of power in determining the extent to which its children will become involved in 'participation' exercises. Those that come from middle class or active working class families are more likely to 'participate'. Young women and men who have not known or seen power and organisation are likely to be excluded from such exercises.

Age plays a powerful role in determining the sort of youth provision young people can expect to experience. It often seems that in the youth workers' minds there are two age categories that involve two different forms of youth work. Thus for the under-14s youth work is largely competition/activity based. Over 14 and we begin to see the trimmings of social education – the attempts at participation, the development of discussions on topics like sex and sexuality, and the use of experiential forms of learning. Such a division cuts right across the developmental needs we examined in the last chapter. In many respects that initial period of adolescence (from 11 to 14 years) involves more change than the later period. It is, after all, in this period that young people have to begin to come to terms with a new set of emotional and physical experiences. It is here that people gain a more sophisticated picture of themselves in the world. Given all this, the way we work with the 11-14 age group seems all the stranger. To deny people the opportunity to have some control over the sort of youth work they receive is a peculiar way of meeting their developmental need for responsibility.

We can see similar patterns in the way we discriminate on ground of gender or race. In the case of gender, for example, in recent years the evidence concerning the way we work with young men and women builds a formidable case for workers to make a major appraisal of their work. Many of us still encourage girls and young women to view their lives in terms of marriage and motherhood. On the other hand our work with boys remains almost totally orientated toward promoting ideas and activities which reinforce sexist attitudes and does little to encourage young men to examine and understand their masculinity.

Similarly, whilst most youth workers would claim that they do not discriminate on the grounds of race, a great deal of youth work can still be said to be racist by default. This is because workers fail to do anything about developing anti racist attitudes. Thus when young people come into youth clubs wearing National Front badges and similar insignia –

---

* John Eggleston, *Adolescence and Community*, Edward Arnold, London, 1976 p109

their presence goes unchallenged. Racist graffiti and symbols get left up on the walls. Jokes about ethnic minorities get laughed at. Here we see workers through their inaction and sometimes through a misplaced desire to be 'one of the boys'(sic), supporting and colluding with racism.

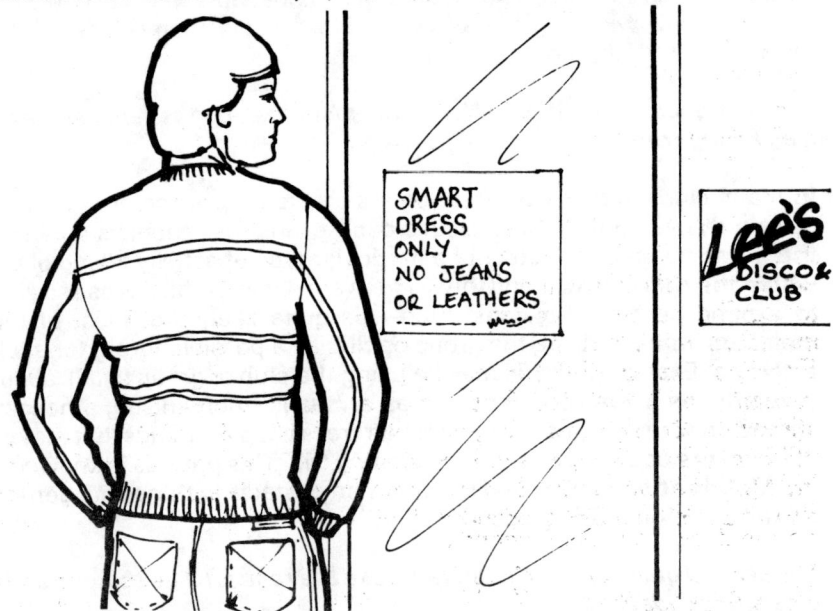

Fifth, workers need to understand the 'politics of the youth group'. In the last section we saw how the subordination process is reproduced in the club or group. We now need to examine how workers themselves 'exclude' young people's wishes.

A useful starting point is our attitude to management committees. The youth workers tells his/her members that they couldn't possibly be full members of the management committee (and so be able to discuss the worker's performance and conditions of employment), because they wouldn't be able to see both sides of the question/wouldn't be able to keep confidences/would be bored by the meetings/and so on. In other words s/he is excluding them and maintaining them in a subordinate position. What response can the members make? They have little access to information and to the sources of power. At a collective level, (if they have the confidence and skills to go that far), deputations appear with demands, teams refuse to play, at a negative level equipment gets smashed, relationships become unpleasant. The saddest outcome is when members actually believe the things the worker says about their abilities and attitudes – they accept the 'rightness' of their powerless position. Here the worker is not simply failing to meet developmental needs but is actively conspiring to block them.

If we go back to our definition of power, we can see that in our examination of the way things happen in youth groups, we should be looking at what gets onto the decision making agenda. An issue has to pass through a number of gateways before a youth worker will answer it directly. Let us consider what might have happened if Neil had been in a different club with a group of workers who saw themselves as the 'providers' and 'deciders'.

The first question is 'Would Neil think about making the request for an ice skating trip?'

In many clubs and groups the workers create an environment around certain issues so that those issues don't even cross people's minds. If there has not been a history of a particular type of activity taking place within the club or group and the workers are not in the business of trying to expand people's horizons, then it is quite likely that most of the members would not see the group or club as a possible forum for such activities. Examples of this may be using the club or group to talk about sexuality, as a live rock venue or as a means of organising a holiday abroad. In some groups it may not even cross people's minds that they or the workers could organise an ice skating trip. This process is known as the **Mobilization of Bias** and is a common obstacle to things not getting on the decision making agenda.

The second question is 'Would Neil make the request if he thought a trip was a good idea?'

Let us assume that the idea of a club skating trip had crossed Neil's mind. The next hurdle is the actual asking of the question. Frequently questions are not asked or demands made because members believe it would be no good if they did. They 'know' in advance that the workers would refuse because they had 'too much work' or some other excuse. Another response might be that they expect the workers to make no response! The request will simply be left unanswered. A third possibility is that members fear for what could happen if they did speak out – they expect a retaliatory response. Members may want to complain because a certain person is excluded from the club but don't speak out because they might be branded as a trouble maker and therefore not 'suitable' for other club activities. This way of stopping an issue reaching the 'agenda' is known as **Anticipating Reactions**.

Question three is 'What happens when Neil does make a request?'

Here the workers may simply fail to directly respond – they say neither yes nor no. Examples of this sort of behaviour are
- not 'hearing' the request
- proposing a delaying course of action e.g. suggesting that a small

Figure 6 **Non-Decision Making**

Three ways of saying no without saying no

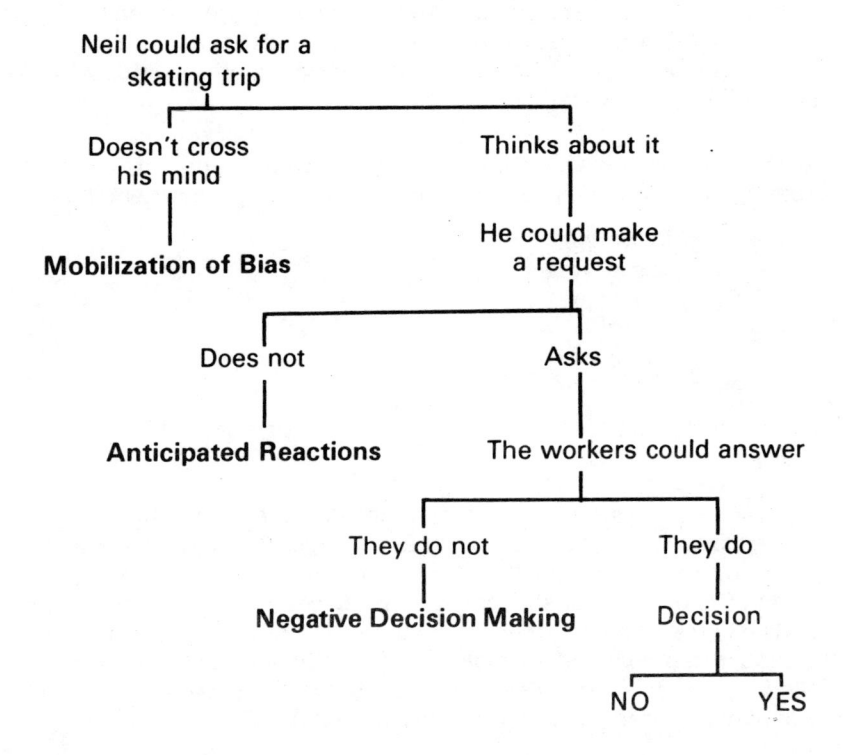

```
            Neil could ask for a
                skating trip
         ┌──────────┴──────────┐
   Doesn't cross          Thinks about it
     his mind                  │
         │              He could make
Mobilization of Bias       a request
                     ┌──────────┴──────────┐
                  Does not               Asks
                     │                     │
            Anticipated Reactions   The workers could answer
                              ┌──────────┴──────────┐
                          They do not            They do
                              │                     │
                     Negative Decision Making    Decision
                                              ┌─────┴─────┐
                                             NO          YES
```

Based on 'The non-decision making filter' in Peter Saunders, *Urban Politics – A sociological interpretation,* London, Penguin 1980 p29.

group should look into the matter (knowing that the whole thing may fizzle out)
• saying the idea sounds interesting and proposing that the person should join the members committee/junior leaders' group so that s/he is brought into the power structure and can be more easily controlled.

This strategy is known as **negative decision making** – where people are able to make a noisy protest but nobody listens.

Lastly, Neil's request may actually get on the 'agenda' and a decision is made.

There is, of course, no guarantee that it will go in his favour. The workers may say no.

This **non-decision making process** is shown diagrammatically in *Figure 6*.

Here, then, we have the process by which issues are filtered out before an actual decision has to be made. We also need to consider the basis on which the worker is able to use his/her power. In other words why does the worker have power?

Much that has been written about the sources of power in social or organisational settings can be brought under six broad headings

- Physical power
- Resource power
- Position power
- Expert power
- Personal power
- Negative power

(The main characteristics of these sources of power are summarised in *Figure 7*).

What such analysis can do is to help us understand the position of workers and what they can do to encourage young people to achieve some control for themselves. Thus, for example, if we apply these headings to the relationship between youth workers and young people, it can be seen that the sources of power most frequently in young people's hands are negative and physical. In saying this we must bear in mind the following points: Firstly, as we have seen, there is power on both 'sides'. Thus what is of interest is the *balance of power.*

Secondly, it is important to be clear where that power can be used. Many of the arguments in organisations are about *boundaries*. What domain can a particular group or individual rule over? Thus whilst the worker may have control over what goes on in certain parts of a club – there may be other parts (such as the toilets!) where his/her control is more marginal and is in dispute.

Lastly, the amount of power an individual or group has will *change* – it is not constant. Changing circumstances, new issues, will put strains on power relationships, bring new forces into play. The power of one group is likely to be discovered a bluff when it fails to deliver the goods.

Understanding the nature of power, how it is used and what is its hidden agenda is of central importance. If youth workers are to seriously make

Figure 7 **Sources of individual power**
There are six possible sources of individual power which give the holder the ability to influence others

Physical Power
This category is self explanatory – it is based on the threat or use of physical coercion. It does not have to be used to be effective – if people believe in its existence and see it as superior to their own power then that will be enough. As a power source it can be particularly significant when adults deal with children, or men with women.

Resource Power
Here the person is in control of resources that others desire. It is also known as 'reward power'. Thus where the youth worker has control over a building and the provision for certain activities then s/he can have considerable power through the threat of withdrawal. Rewards need not be material. They can be things like the granting of status.

Position Power
This power comes through a particular role or position in an organisation. Position gives the holder authority to do certain things. It is sometimes called 'legal' or 'legitimate power' and in the end has to be underwritten by either physical or resource power. Position power gives the holder potential control over some crucial 'unseen' assets.

- *Information.* Information is usually directed towards a particular position such as 'youth worker' or 'secretary'.
- *Right of access.* Positions give entry to a variety of networks. Committee membership is often ex officio. People in other organisations will often only 'listen' to those holding a certain level of position.
- *The right to organise.* Position confers on the holder the right to different behaviours – s/he controls the way work is organised, the layout of the physical and social environment, the way decisions are made, and so on.

Expert Power
Expert power is vested in someone because of his/her acknowledged expertise. It is only influential for as long as it is recognised that the holder has expertise. In a 'meritocratic' society it is a power that many will accept. Only if expertise is

> questioned do the holders have to resort to other sources of power to get their recommendations accepted.
>
> **Personal Power**
> Also known as 'charisma', here power resides in the person and in his/her personality. It can be enhanced by a person's expertise or position. Personal power is tied to success and self-confidence and can quickly disappear in defeat. Many people make the mistake of viewing their power as being personal rather than positional.
>
> **Negative Power**
> All the previous forms of power are 'legitimate' in particular situations. If power is used contrary to the agreed rules then it could be said to be negative power. Negative power is, therefore, the ability to stop things happening, to delay them, to distort them. In a sense this power is an 'illegitimate' use of some of the other forms e.g. of position.
>
> (Based on Charles B Handy, *Understanding Organisations,* London Penguin 1981 (Chapter 5).

in their work a space for young people to gain some understanding, confidence and skills in affecting the political forces that structure their lives, then the problem of power has to be tackled. This whole discussion points to the need to face up to the way we keep things off the decision making agenda. How do we, as workers, contribute to young people's powerlessness?

Sixth, we must look for the possibilities for action.
The problem with the sort of questions that have been raised here is that they run very deep. Confronting our own racism or sexism can be *personally* very threatening. For instance, as a male youth worker when I begin to examine the way I work with young women and girls it doesn't stop with questions about the relative range of activities available to them, but has to explore the way I relate to them, what sort of things do we talk about, what sort of attitudes am I communicating? I am then faced with questions about my relationship with women workers in the group. Are they doing 'women's work' – looking after the domestic side, the relationships, leaving the men to 'organise'? This questioning then leads to my own family relationships. Do I do my share of the housework, cooking or childcare? Is the responsibility for these equally shared? Whose interests are paramount when we make decisions? How do I use the peculiar and 'unsocial' nature of youth work to avoid family responsibilities and so on? It doesn't even stop there. I then have to start

person's life are affected by factors such as class, race, gender and age then the significance of these concepts can be grasped. The problem of course, is that education has generally been seen as passive. People sit behind desks in rows and learn. As soon as they leave the classroom and think and act on that learning then this is somehow not education. The problems multiply when we consider what sort of things might go to make up the **skills** part of a political education curriculum.

The ice skating trip shows a considerable cross-over between the concerns of a more traditional social education and the aims of a developmental needs or critical approach. A clear implication of the analysis in this chapter is that action on the political system involves action in groups. As individuals, we have (or *feel* we have), little chance or power to get things changed. The achievement of power for all members of society involves collective action. In this sense social education's traditional emphasis on groups, collective and participative ways of working, and the development of the necessary knowledge, feelings and skills for groups to work echoes the contents of a political curriculum. However, what is different is that a developmental needs approach indicates a far more active involvement by workers and young people in the creation of space to be able to do things for themselves. This involves action on the political system. The skills involved are not just the inter personal/communication skills of groupwork but the skills of political action – lobbying, organising public meetings, and so on.*

A growing number of workers have discovered the difficulties likely to be faced with managers and employers when they begin work in this area. It is rather more of a problem for full-time workers. Employers (local councillors and their officers) are not known for their charity towards employees who appear to be questioning and challenging decisions they have made. Particularly where this challenge is public. Even where workers have remained within a strictly educational role, their giving of help to those who question their employers policies and actions, brings conflict. There is a sense in which this is inevitable. Social education, if it means anything to local councillors, is likely to be seen as a form of control. The values we have discussed lead to a form of education markedly different.

When we come to the **feelings** area of the curriculum a similar crossover between traditional and critical approaches is there. The inter personal values have to be translated into political values (as we did in 'The politics of developmental needs'). The feeling of personal confidence and worth becomes a sense of solidarity and worth as a group. This identification of the individual with the group is a crucial part of politics.

---

* A full description of these skills and much of the relevant knowledge can be found in *Organise!*

In many respects it is this area that can cause most problems for youth workers with their managers. For what this entails, if we are to follow the logic of our analysis, is for people to define themselves in terms of their gender, race, age and class. Over the last few years much of the political action taken by young people from within a Youth Service context has been by groups who have a close identity with one or more of these factors. Thus we have seen young Black and Asian groups campaigning for improved youth provision, organising around issues such as police harrassment and developing a wide range of self help organisations. Similarly we have lately witnessed a mushrooming of activities by groups of young women – the production of magazines both local and national, putting pressure on for increased 'girls only' provision and so on. The importance of what has been happening in both these areas of youth work is that in practice very clear linkages have been made between young people's everyday experience and the characteristics by which they are oppressed – their race, gender and age.

To a certain extent both these areas of work have been allowed to develop within a Youth Service context because they can exploit the (white, male) liberal guilt of those who administer the service. The 'solution' that administrators have proposed – multicultural mixed youth work – has been found to be wanting. It has been rejected by many of the young people it was supposedly designed for. A vacuum was created – the Youth Service had no real answer to this rejection yet felt something had to be done. This space has to some extent been filled by workers and groups of young people who defined themselves first and foremost as 'Black' or 'Female'. However their success, whilst being significant, is also limited. The direction and form of their work has been experienced as threatening by both administrators and workers. In a sense there is little that can be done about this as the work should be threatening. It should be challenging the racism and sexism that permeates our society.

Beyond youth work defined by gender and race stands a form of work that has not been able to exploit the guilt of those who run the Youth Service – youth work defined by class. If we accept that social education should be about helping people to understand their relationship to power and to know who else might be in the same boat, then class has to be tackled. Developing people's consciousness of class and the way their membership of a particular class affects their ideas and life chances can lead workers into difficult areas. However the next two steps – developing people's *identity* with a particular class and *taking action* on that understanding – are such that it is difficult to conceive of many situations where state sponsored youth work could handle such activities. How many local authorities would agree to their employees encouraging young people to identify with the 'excluded' class and to undertake collective action i.e. the achievement of power for the group or class as a whole? Such a form of youth work, with values and an analysis which lead to conflict, makes clear the controlling functions of traditional youth work. It is at this point that social education's values clash with political reality, where politicians' fine words and phrases dissolve into one – NO!

So what can social educators do? If they try to push a conflict model of work too far within a state sponsored Youth Service then their money and jobs will soon be lost. If social educators try to forget or skate round the issue their morality has to be questioned. Perhaps the only realistic course is for workers to recognise, that as such a form of social education is oppositional, it must largely take place outside the state sector. It has to be 'voluntary'. That said, much can still be done from within the statutory sector and its satellites to support the efforts of those attempting a more critical form of social education.

This then, is some of the ground that an exploration of the possibilities for action must cover. As suggested in the opening paragraphs such an exploration is far from comfortable. It includes looking at one's personal life, examining the means by which we hold on to power, defining what might be part of a critical social education curriculum. Finally and inevitably it leaves a number of questions about just how far such a form of youth work can be pursued from within a state run youth service.

Seventh, workers need to be sure of their ground before proceeding
As we have seen, workers that have developed a more critical form of social education work have frequently found themselves in difficulties both with their employers and with the work they have begun. In our experience four broad problem areas have arisen.

i. *The failure to act politically.* Many attempts in this area have been rather naive. As has been suggested here social education is political and a critical social education is Political with a big 'P'. Whilst much of the knowledge and skill involved is that traditionally associated with youth work, the activity surrounding the creation of space for this sort of work involves conscious political action. It involves the creation of links with other organisations and bodies that can support and legitimise the work. The creation of strong and supportive management committees. The convincing of councillors and administrators of the importance and legitimacy of **the work.**

Making the work *legitimate* and gaining strength through *acting collectively* are the two main themes that workers will have to tackle if they are to develop a more critical form of social education. Whilst this conflicts with the 'spontaneous' ethos of much of youth work, it is very necessary if workers are to avoid the mistakes of the past.

ii. *The failure to act educationally.* It must not be forgotten that the base from which this work springs is an *educational* one. This means that any interventions with young people have to governed by the sort of values that were discussed in the last chapter. Thus the work must be open, truthful, enhancing of the persons freedom and dignity. Rather too often, workers have got off on a 'trip' of their own. Too often workers have seen themselves as advocates professing to speak for young people rather than directing their efforts into helping people to develop skills for themselves or have allowed their own unworked through feelings to cloud their response to young people's needs.

Whilst the relationship between workers and young people has to be educational, the relationship between the worker and his/her managers is beset with a number of dilemmas. For instance, just how open can, or should, a worker be, given what we have already said about political naivety? There is a need to educate managers and employers but this has to be set alongside the creation of political pressure to support the work you wish to develop. Getting this particular balance right is no easy matter.

iii. *The failure to act professionally.* I'm rather hesitant about using the word 'profesional' as I've always felt that it is a singularly inappropriate way of describing the position and relationship of a youth worker with the young people s/he works with. Perhaps 'craftspersonship' is more appropriate. Whatever, quite a number of problems arise through workers not working out objectives for their work, planning appropriate actions and responses and evaluating what they are doing. The process outlined in Chapter 1 of assessing – planning – executing – evaluating applies equally to the workers organisation of his/her time as to solving a particular problem.

iv. *The failure to recognise the constraints of the working situation.* Just how much can be achieved in a particular working situation varies from area to area. Workers need to make a careful assessment of just what is possible. If circumstances (and employers in particular) mean that the sort of work you want to engage in will be seriously compromised then it is likely to be better to pursue the work outside a formal youth work context. In other words it has to be done in your own time. Thus groups of workers have used organisations such as their local union branch, local voluntary organisations or groups set up specifically for the purpose to sponsor their work.

Interestingly some of the most progressive work has occurred where workers have a high degree of accountability to their employers. They have used reports and detailed plans in order to get their work accepted by their employers whilst at the same time building up a strong political base for their work. Their secret (if they have one) has in general been to start small, to gain credibility and then to build on that.

Eighth, Act!
Whilst there are very real problems in extending and exploring social education work, there is a tendency for workers to see ghosts. Problems that are in reality marginal gain an importance in workers' minds that blocks the development of their work. As we have seen it is necessary to be realistic about the prospects but there are gaps and spaces within the Youth Service that can be exploited. In many respects it is the first step into a critical practice that is the most difficult one. Once taken, bits of the jigsaw begin to fall into place, and possibilities appear for a more creative and critical social education.

In conclusion
For too long youth workers have tried or pretended to be neutral or non-political. In any society where injustice remains, the social educator has to take sides. As Paulo Freire once wrote

"Washing one's hands of the conflict between the powerful and the powerless means to side with the powerful, not to be neutral."

Sadly, through our failure to recognise that social education involves action at both an individual and a collective level, we have taken sides **with the powerful.**

Will we change?

Afterword – Towards a critical social education?

Looking back over the last chapter one word seems to spring out from the pages – the word **critical**. Its arrival is no accident. Three meanings of the word join together and make its use important.

First, much social education has been uncritical of the society and time it has been born of. It has accepted the powerless position of those it is supposed to help and done little to change that situation, even though this would appear to be a direct contradiction of its core values. In an unjust society social education has to be critical.

Second, there is a lack of good theory around in youth work. Rather too much reliance is placed on 'what worked last week'. This folk or practice wisdom needs careful criticism and examination. If social education is to develop and have meaning it must connect its practice with theory. It must develop a careful or critical analysis.

Third, our society is currently in a time of abrupt change and crisis. Gaps are widening and old solutions are not working. Youth workers need a theory and a practice that speaks to such critical times.

In a sense it should be unnecessary to put the word **critical** in front of the phrase 'social education', for what is education if it is not a critical process? Unfortunately much of what passes for social education neither questions nor develops, and it is because workers and managers have so debased the concept that the word critical becomes so important.

Helping people to meet developmental needs must involve educators in politics and in making plain the values and assumptions that inform their work. Personal problems and experiences can only be fully understood and acted upon when they are seen as **both** private 'troubles' and public issues. This is the task for a critical social education and whilst the problems are formidable, the opportunity for action is always with us. The starting point can be as close as a member's request for you to organise a trip and the readiness on your part to encourage and help them to do the thing for themselves. Neil's request may not have seemed very special, but the fact that he ended up a creator rather than a mere consumer is not without personal and political significance.

Further Reading

I have only listed books or articles that I feel are particularly helpful. Anybody who wants detailed references should contact me c/o NAYC Publications.

1. Bernard Davies : **Part-time Youth Work in an Industrial Community**
   Leicester : National Youth Bureau, 1976.

   : **In Whose Interests? From Social Education to Social and Life Skills Training**
   Leicester : National Youth Bureau, 1979.

   In the 1976 pamphlet Bernard Davies reflects on 7 years part-time youth work and tries to set the personal and individual focus of his work in its wider social and political context. *In Whose Interests* provides a critique of recent developments in social skills training and the impact of economic and political factors on youth work.

2. P Priestly, J McGuire, D Flegg, V Hemsley and D Welham :
   Social Skills & Personal Problem Solving
   London, Tavistock 1978

   This book presents a practical approach to helping people, individually or in groups, to identify and then cope better with some of the problems they face using a wide range of social skills and problem solving methods.

3. John C Coleman : **The Nature of Adolescence**
London, Methuen 1980

A good summary of the current state of adolescent psychology.

4. David W Johnson and Frank P Johnson :
Joining Together - Group Therapy and Group Skills
New Jersey, Prentice Hall 1975

The book attempts to provide "an experiential approach to learning about the social psychology of groups and to developing the skills needed to function effectively in groups". Used in conjunction with Alan Brown, **Groupwork**, London, Heinemann, 1979, it provides an excellent introduction to groupwork practice.

5. C Wright Mills : **The Sociological Imagination**
Harmsworth, Penguin Books 1970

An introduction to the insights a sociological perspective can provide.

6. **Schooling and Culture, Issue 9**
London, ILEA Cockpit Arts Workshop, Spring 1981

This issue, *Youth, Community: Crisis*, includes a number of relevant articles. See in particular, Mica Nava, *Girls aren't really a problem...*, Tony Taylor and Roy Ratcliffe, *Stuttering steps in political education*, and Bernard Davies, *Social Education and Political Education: In Search of Integration*.

7. Mark Smith : **Organise! A guide to practical politics for youth and community groups**
Leicester, NAYC Publications, 1981.

Part 1 of this book describes a way of working and making decisions in groups that is both personal and democratic. Part 2 provides a step by step approach to getting information. Part 3 is a comprehensive guide to taking action. It includes sections on getting members, lobbying, using the press, organising petitions and public meetings and the other activities of politics.

8. Maury Smith : **A Practical Guide to Value Clarification**
    La Jolla, University Associates, 1977.

In the early seventies there was quite a growth in 'values' literature in the States. This particular guide contains a brief introduction to the idea, 29 structured experiences, and a short but useful chapter on designing value clarification programmes. Also included are a number of readings of variable utility and a select bibliography.
(Available from University Associates, 45 Victoria Street, Mansfield, Notts. NG18 5GU)

9. Sidney B Simon, Leland W Howe, Howard Kirschenbaum
    Values Clarification: A Handbook of Practical Strategies for Teachers and Students
    New York, Hart Publishing, 1972.

This handbook contains 79 structured exercises, primarily for use in schools (both primary and secondary). Also included are suggestions for the use of the techniques.
(Available from Dillons University Bookshop Ltd., 1 Malet St. London WC1)

10. NYB Youth Work Unit
    Enfranchisement: young people and the law – An information pack for youth workers
    Leicester, NYB, 1981.

The pack contains a wide range of material concerning legislation and the issues that arise from it.

11. NAYC Girls Work: **Girls Work Pack**
    Leicester, NAYC Publications, 1981.

This pack contains reports from various projects and events, background briefing papers and an introduction. Two other excellent publications from Girls Work are the **Working with Girls Newsletter** and **Girls can do anything** – a set of nine posters.

12 **Waiting our turn**
    Belfast, NIAYC, 1981.

Produced in Northern Ireland, this book provides a step by step introduction into setting up and running a girls group.

13. Judy H Katz : **White Awareness – A handbook for anti-racism training**
    Oklahoma, University of Oklahoma Press, 1978.

White Awareness, after an introductory section on racism and relations training, offers a detailed and practical training programme plus a listing of readings and materials.
(Available from Housmans, 5 Caledonian Road, Kings Cross, London N1)

14. Charles B Handy: **Understanding Organisations**
London, Penguin Education, 1981.

A good introduction to basic organisational concepts and problems. It includes sections on leadership, power, roles, culture and the workings of groups. The tone and direction of the book are practical and the text includes a substantial number of exercises and examples.

15. Warren Redman: **Guidelines for finding your own support**
Leicester, NAYC Publications, 1981.

A short but very useful guide for workers to different methods of support with suggestions for carrying the guidelines into action.